Milan, fashion and economic capital of Italy as well as one of the richest and most avant-garde metropolises in the world. However, Milan is also art and culture, shopping and high society, hospitality and good food. The pedestrian street running from Sforzesco Castle to San Babila and continuing on to Via Montenapoleone, renders a visit to the city even more charming. Along the way you will see V.I.Ps, models, businessmen and tourists from all over the world, who never tire of admiring the Duomo, a world famous masterpiece. The Last Supper by Leonardo Da Vinci, the Scala Theatre, the "Navigli", the Basilica of Sant'Ambrogio, the Meazza Stadium and much, much more make this city worth visiting and discovering: you will never know Italy until you have visited Milan.

Summary

A BRIEF HISTORY

From the foundation of the city to Sant'Ambrogio

According to the legend told by the historical Latin figure Tito Livio, the establishment of the Mediolanum (the old name for Milan) took place in around 600 BC lead by the Gallics, who settled in the middle of the Padan plain (or the Po valley) after defeating the Etruscans. In 222 BC, the Roman Legion was conquered and, due to its strategic position, was extremely important in Julius Caesar's campaign to overthrow the Gallics between 58 and 50 BC. There are very few traces left of the Roman era, enough however, to show that the public buildings were part of a great and prosperous city, which became capital of the Roman Empire in 292 AD. In 313 AD, Emperor Constantine issued the famous "Edict of Milan", a fundamental date for Christianity since it was the first time that freedom to worship had been granted.

Sant'Ambrogio was born in Treviri in 330 AD and after finishing his studies in Rome, he was sent to Milan to be a governor. There, he was acclaimed Bishop by the population and became one of the most important political figures at the time. When he died in 397, he was declared Patron Saint of the city, which, in the meantime, had become one of the most influential centres of Christianity.

Following the fall of Rome in 476 AD, even Milan, like the rest of Europe, was plundered by the barbarians, thrown into chaos and decline.

1 – A statue of Emperor Constantine in front of the Basilica of San Lorenzo
2 – Basilica of Sant'Ambrogio

From the Lombard League to the Spanish Rule

The slow recovery began in the 8th century with the rule of the successors of Carlo Magno. In 1176 Milan, strong once again, became headquarters for the Lombard League that overthrew the German Emperor Federico Barbarossa and reclaimed the powerful role it once held. In 1300 a new city wall was built as well as a system of canals known as the "Navigli", that still outline the features of the city. The first stone of the Duomo was also laid in that period (1386) and its construction was completed five centuries later. At the end of the 1200s the Visconti family began to assert itself and the Sforza family arrived in the mid-1400s. As a result, a lot of important people made their way to Milan including Leonardo Da

Vinci, Donato Bramante, bringing about the beginning of the building of Sforzesco Castle, the Church of Santa Maria delle Grazie (St. Mary of Grace) and the Hospital

(today the state university), turning Milan into one of the most important cultural centres of the European Renaissance. However, in 1535 the Spanish oppressive rule began, lasting 170 years and rendered even more difficult because of the plagues that ravished the population. The most dramatic was the plague of 1630, described in the most famous novel in Italian literature, "I Promessi Sposi" (The Betrothed) by the milanese, Alessandro Manzoni.

3 – Sforzesco Castle
4 – Maggiore Hospital also known as "Ca' Granda"

From Napoleon Bonaparte to the Unification of Italy

The Austrians over threw the Spanish at the beginning of the 1700s, which started a period of quick recovery, above all during the period of Maria Teresa. The Brera Accademy was founded and the Scala Theatre, Palazzo Reale (Royal Palace), Villa Reale (Royal Villa) and many other neoclassic buildings were constructed. In the mid-1700s the city counted 108,000 inhabitants. The French Revolution in 1789 and the war that followed brought Milan under the control of the French and Napoleon Bonaparte, who made it the capital of the Cisalpine Republic, reinstating its cultural and economic importance. There followed a brief period of intense ideological and artistic fervour which gave the city, alongside the first regulatory urbanisation plans, incredible structures like the Arena and the "Nuove Porte" (New Doors). The Duomo, where Napoleon wanted to be crowned in 1805, was also completed. With the end of Napoleon Bonaparte in 1815, Milan returned to the dominion of the Austrians, much to the dislike of the population and the upper classes: the discontent finally leaded to a bloody uprising known as the "Cinque Giornate di Milano" (Five Days of Milan). However, the desire for independence and the unification

of the Italian peninsula became even stronger a few years later and in 1861 a change in the international scene brought about political unification and the proclamation of a Kingdom of Italy.

1 – Statue of Napoleon in Brera
2 – The Scala Theatre

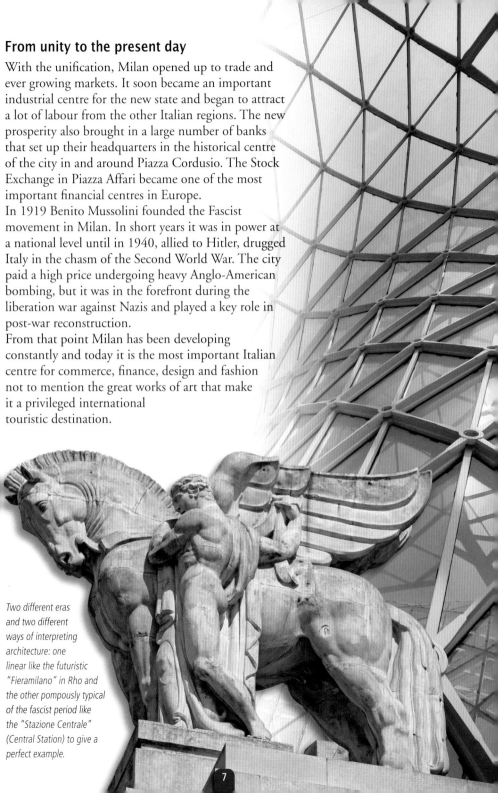

From unity to the present day

With the unification, Milan opened up to trade and ever growing markets. It soon became an important industrial centre for the new state and began to attract a lot of labour from the other Italian regions. The new prosperity also brought in a large number of banks that set up their headquarters in the historical centre of the city in and around Piazza Cordusio. The Stock Exchange in Piazza Affari became one of the most important financial centres in Europe.

In 1919 Benito Mussolini founded the Fascist movement in Milan. In short years it was in power at a national level until in 1940, allied to Hitler, drugged Italy in the chasm of the Second World War. The city paid a high price undergoing heavy Anglo-American bombing, but it was in the forefront during the liberation war against Nazis and played a key role in post-war reconstruction.

From that point Milan has been developing constantly and today it is the most important Italian centre for commerce, finance, design and fashion not to mention the great works of art that make it a privileged international touristic destination.

Two different eras and two different ways of interpreting architecture: one linear like the futuristic "Fieramilano" in Rho and the other pompously typical of the fascist period like the "Stazione Centrale" (Central Station) to give a perfect example.

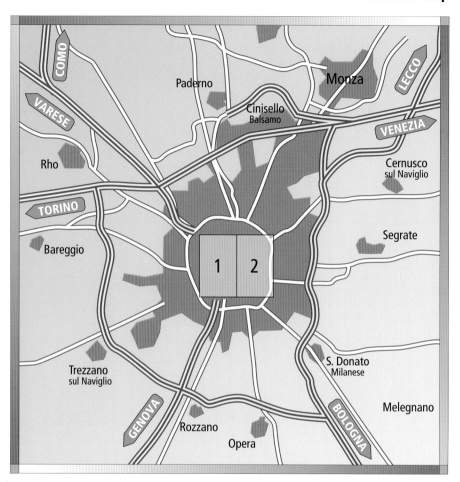

Territory and population

Milan is situated in the heart of the Padan plain and is the main city in Lombardy, the most developed and populated region in Italy with nearly 10 million inhabitants. It is at an altitude of 120 metres above sea level, covers a surface area of 182 km² and its main sources of water are from the Olona, the Lambro and the Seveso not to mention the canals that run through it like the Naviglio Grande (main canal), the Naviglio Pavese, the Naviglio Martesana, the Vettabbia Canal and the Redefossi Canal. The city is home to 1,300,000 inhabitants that reach 3,700,000 if the provincial territory is included. There are a lot of highways that run to and from Milan that hold regional, national and international importance: it is connected to Turin, Genoa, Bologna-Florence, Brescia-Verona-Venice, the Valtellina alpine roads, the Canton Ticino and the Sempione Pass. In the area surrounding Milan there is the most important airport system in Italy including Malpensa, Linate and Orio al Serio airports. Together, every year, they deal with about 30 million passengers.

Map 1

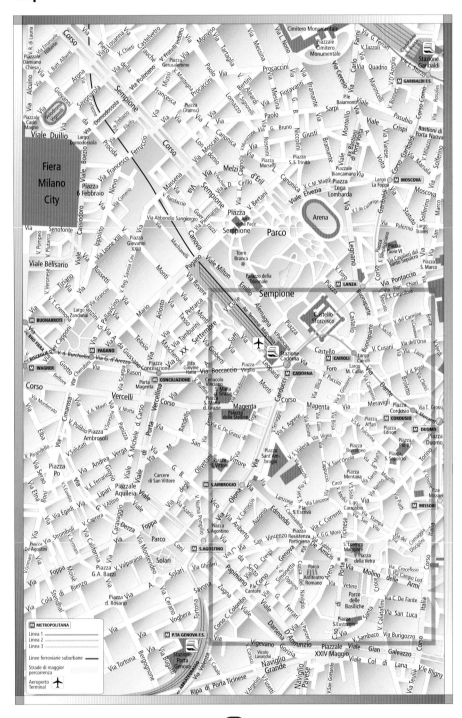

Map 2

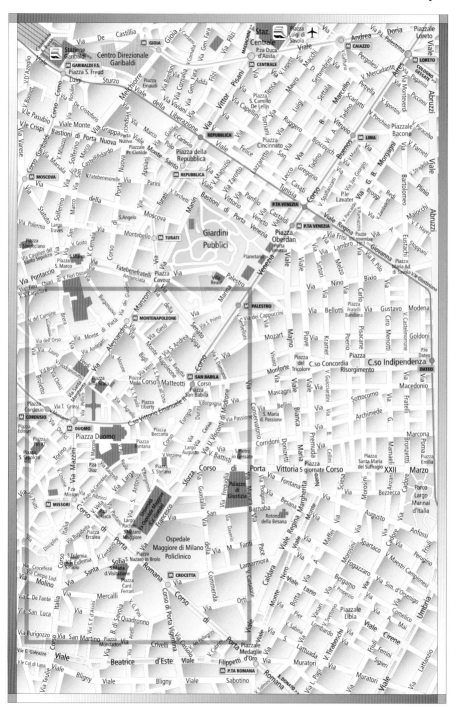

The centre – Map 1

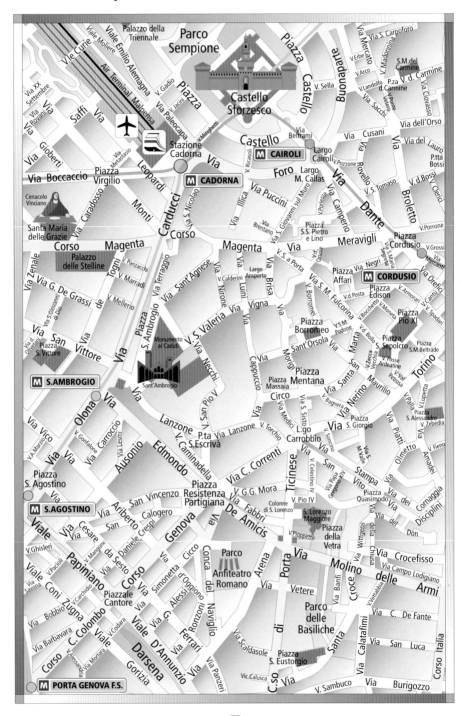

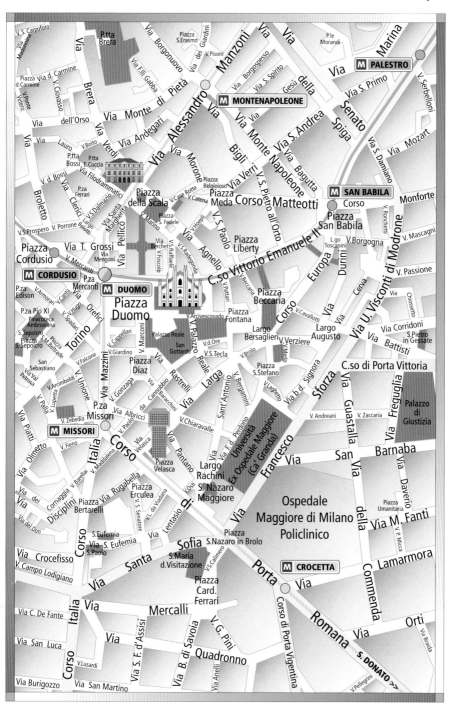

The Underground lines

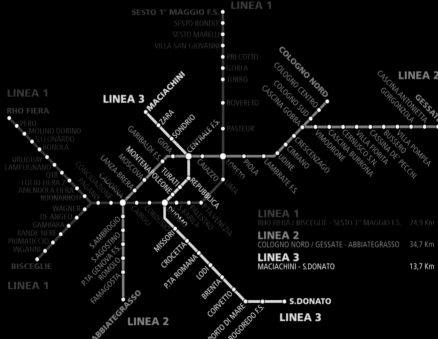

LINEA 1

SESTO 1° MAGGIO F.S.
SESTO RONDO
SESTO MARELLI
VILLA SAN GIOVANNI
PRECOTTO
GORLA
TURRO
ROVERETO
PASTEUR

LINEA 1

RHO FIERA
PERO
MOLINO DORINO
S.LEONARDO
BONOLA
URUGUAY
LAMPUGNANO
QT8
LOTTO FIERA 2
AMENDOLA FIERA
BUONARROTI
WAGNER
DE ANGELI
GAMBARA
BANDE NERE
PRIMATICCIO
INGANNI
BISCEGLIE

LINEA 1

LINEA 3 MACIACHINI
ZARA
SONDRIO
GIOIA
GARIBALDI F.S.
CENTRALE F.S.
LANZA-BRERA
MONTENAPOLEONE
MOSCOVA
TURATI
CAIAZZO
LORETO
PIOLA
LIMA
REPUBBLICA
CONCILIAZIONE
CADORNA
PAGANO
CAIROLI
CORDUSIO
DUOMO
S.BABILA
P.TA VENEZIA
PALESTRO
S.AMBROGIO
S.AGOSTINO
P.TA GENOVA F.S.
ROMOLO
MISSORI
CROCETTA
LODI
P.TA ROMANA
BRENTA
CORVETTO
FAMAGOSTA
PORTO DI MARE
ROGOREDO F.S.

ABBIATEGRASSO

LINEA 2

COLOGNO NORD

COLOGNO CENTRO
COLOGNO SUD
CASCINA GOBBA
CRESCENZAGO
CIMIANO
UDINE
LAMBRATE F.S.
VIMODRONE

LINEA 2

CASCINA ANTONIETTA
GORGONZOLA
GESSATE
VILLA POMPEA
BUSSERO
CASSINA DE' PECCHI
VILLA FIORITA
CERNUSCO S.N.
CASCINA BURRONA

LINEA 1
RHO FIERA / BISCEGLIE - SESTO 1° MAGGIO F.S.   24,9 Km

LINEA 2
COLOGNO NORD / GESSATE - ABBIATEGRASSO   34,7 Km

LINEA 3
MACIACHINI - S.DONATO   13,7 Km

S.DONATO

LINEA 3

14

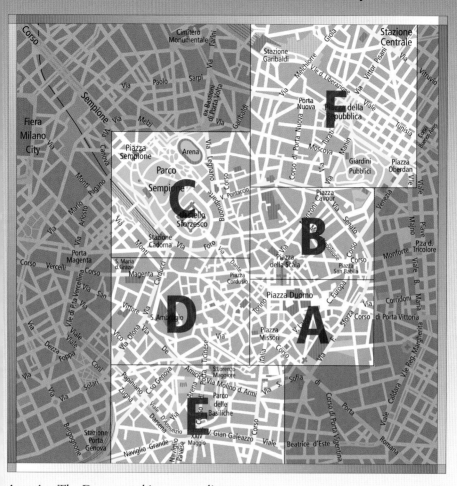

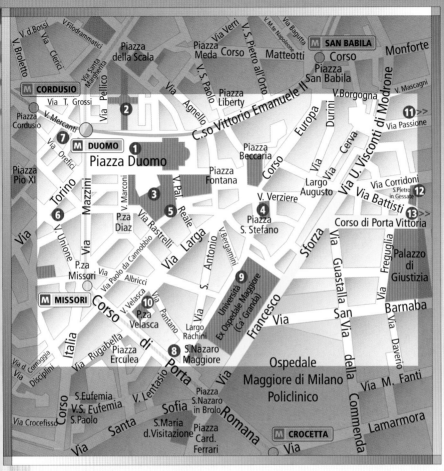

Piazza del Duomo

This is the heart of Milan, the centre of the city's entire urban fabric. The typical Italian square is rectangular in shape and was renovated in 1859 based on a project by Giuseppe Mengoni. All the buildings and spaces were positioned with the Duomo in mind, the key feature that closes the view at the end of the square. In the middle there is an equestrian statue of Vittorio Emanuele II, created by Ercole Rosa in 1896, which shows the sovereign pulling on the reigns of his horse and turning towards his troops, stirring them up for the battle of San Martino in 1859. Along both sides of the square there are porticoed buildings: Palazzo Settentrionale with its monumental entrance into the Vittorio Emanuele II Gallery; Palazzo Meridionale followed by two smaller buildings, the "Propilei", built in 1939 demonstrate the coldness of the architecture of that time compared to the classic linearity of Palazzo Reale (Royal Palace), which is adjacent to the little square. Palazzo dell'Orologio (Clock Palace) is on the west side. Even underneath the square one can find hidden treasures that were brought to light during the building of the underground system in 1942, like the findings of the ancient Basilica di Santa Tecla from the 4th century and the remains of Santa Maria Maggiore that gave up its place for the impressive Duomo.

The Duomo (Cathedral)

This is the symbol of the city, impressive and spectacular not only due to its size (157m long and 93m wide) but also to its fascinating structure. It represents the most extraordinary example of Italian "flamboyant gothic". Its construction, which was started in 1386 and lasted 5 centuries, involved both Italian and European architects and artists. Despite the length of its completion it didn't lose any of its original homogeneity rendering it one of the most renowned and complex gothic buildings in the world. This is also thanks to the use of technical solutions in its construction that had never been put in practice before. Built entirely out of Candoglia marble (near Lago Maggiore) transported to the city using the "Navigli" (canals), it is decorated with more than 3200 statues, hundreds of spires, pinnacles and gargoyles. On the main spire there is a 4-metre-high golden statue of the Madonnina (Virgin Mary). Inside one can find a large number of valuable sculptures done in a wide range of materials: marble, bronze, wood and glass. Splendid are the huge stained-glass windows with about 3600 reproduced scenes. The main door by Ludovico Pogliani (early 1900s) is impressive and it is traditionally believed to be good luck to touch the leg of the figure in the right-hand panel. The view of the city and the Alps from the terrace is also breathtaking.

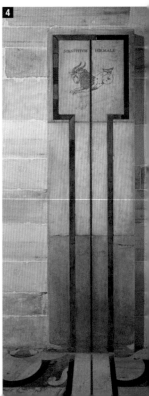

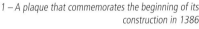

1 – A plaque that commemorates the beginning of its construction in 1386

2 – The crypt in which the remains of San Carlo Borromeo are conserved

3 – Statue of San Bartolomeo Scorticato (skinned San Bartolomeo)

4 – Near the entrance, on the floor, one can see a brass strip that re-emerges on the North wall. It's the famous Sundial of the Duomo. On the South wall, at a height of 24 m, there is a hole through which a ray of light is projected on to the strip on the floor at midday. On each side of the metal line there are marble tiles that depict the signs of the zodiac

5 – Original Roman Baptismal Font

6/7 – Beautiful stained-glass windows from the 1500s

8 – Details of the marble floor

The "Madonnina"

In the 18th century, the Duomo was still lacking a little in spires and so the Archbishop, Giuseppe Pozzobonelli, decided to raise the main spire. The work was completed in 1769 by the architect Francesco Croce reaching 108.5 metres. A 4.16 metre, gilded copper statue of Our Lady of the Assumption was placed at the top. The statue is affectionately called the "Madonnina" and is holding her arms and her face towards heaven as if she were asking for God's blessing on the city for which she has become a symbol. The statue was created by Giuseppe Perego and the goldsmith Giuseppe Bini and was unveiled on December 30, 1774.

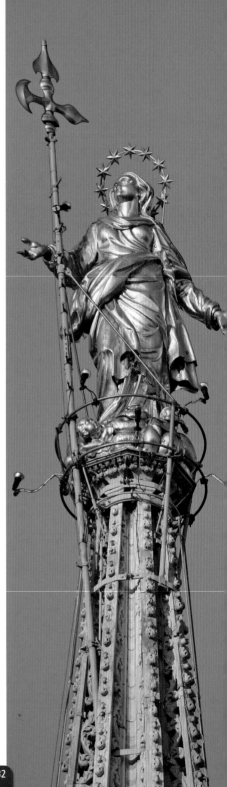

A view of the Duomo and the Branca Tower

Vittorio Emanuele II Gallery

Designed by the architect Giuseppe Mengoni (1865-1877), this was one of the first structures built in iron and glass. It is in the shape of a cross with an octagonal "piazza" in the centre covered by a 47 metre-high dome. Two intersecting arms, one 105 and the other 196 metres long and both 14 metres wide meet in the "piazza".

It is rich in decoration (frescoes, stucco, marble and plaster). Today it is known as "The living room of Milan", a favourite meeting place for residents and tourists. Inside one can enjoy the elegant shops, cafés, restaurants and book shops, and in some of these original decorations and furniture can still be seen.

Inside the Gallery
there are Coats of
Arms of Turin. There is
a superstitious ritual
involving the bull that is
connected to granting
good luck to visitors, as
you can see in the photo

Vittorio Emanuele II Gallery

Palazzo Reale (Royal Palace)

Palazzo Reale (see photo above) was built in 1138 on top of the Broletto Vecchio, the old town hall. Later on it became home to the Torriani, the Visconti and the Sforza families. It hosted the Governors of Spain and at one point it was also the first permanent theatre in the city. In 1772, the architect Piermarini was given the task of renovating the building by Ferdinando d'Austria. Important modifications were carried out and illustrious Italian and foreign artists were called in to decorate and enrich the interior. It was heavily damaged during the bombardments of 1943 and all the frescoes on the vaulted ceilings were destroyed. Thanks to painstaking restoration the sober neoclassic façade can again be admired. Today it is host to museums and temporary exhibitions.

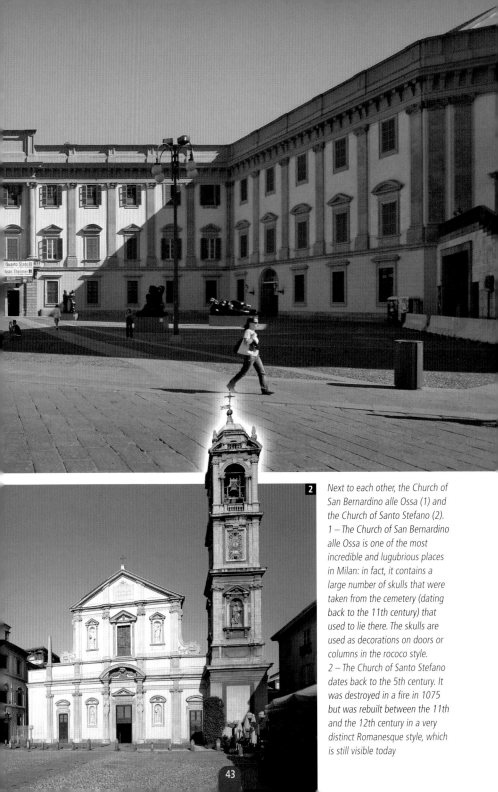

2 Next to each other, the Church of San Bernardino alle Ossa (1) and the Church of Santo Stefano (2).

1 – The Church of San Bernardino alle Ossa is one of the most incredible and lugubrious places in Milan: in fact, it contains a large number of skulls that were taken from the cemetery (dating back to the 11th century) that used to lie there. The skulls are used as decorations on doors or columns in the rococo style.

2 – The Church of Santo Stefano dates back to the 5th century. It was destroyed in a fire in 1075 but was rebuilt between the 11th and the 12th century in a very distinct Romanesque style, which is still visible today

Piazza Fontana

Church of San Gottardo

Azzone Visconti had this church built in 1336 and dedicated it to San Gottardo because he himself suffered from gout. Today one can admire its neoclassic interior and an incredible octagonal bell tower (right-hand photo).

The Verziere Column in Largo Augusto, is a baroque monument built around 1500. It is made up of an elaborate granite column which finishes in a large statue representing "Christ the Redemptor". It gets its name "Verziere" from the vegetable market that used to take place there

Below, Piazza Diaz, created in 1939 after the demolition of some old buildings. In the middle, a monument dedicated to the Carabinieri from 1980

the church despite the meager space that was available to him. It was under these conditions that he managed, with great craftsmanship, to create a sense of perspective by playing with arches and coffered ceilings. The result is a masterpiece of optical illusion with regard to the fake apse, seemingly large and spacious but in reality only 1 metre deep. At the back there is an image of the Mary with Jesus: according to legend, in 1200 someone hit the painting and blood started to flow from the damaged area.

Church of Santa Maria presso San Satiro

Dedicated to the brother of Sant'Ambrogio, the original nucleus of the church dates back to 879 AD, even if the current set up is a Donato Bramante's work (1476-1478) who, at the point of starting the work, discovered he didn't have the necessary documentation to carry on and decided to accept the challenge of building

Via Orefici (1) and Via Mercanti (2) connect Piazza del Duomo and Piazza Cordusio

3 – The Baroque Church of San Giorgio al Palazzo with a 17th century façade situated in Via Torino

4 – Via Torino, full of shops, studios and workshops, has a strong business history mainly because of its favourable position. It is, in fact, situated among the oldest streets in Milan that connect Piazza del Duomo with the historical city centre, from Porta Ticinese to the canal zone. The streets and the side alleys, the main roads in Medieval times, are nearly all in their original state

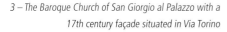

Piazza Mercanti

A beautiful little piazza onto which face the most important public buildings from medieval times. On one side there is the 13th century "Palazzo della Ragione", next door the 17th century "Palazzo delle Scuole Palatine", and in front the "Loggia degli

Osii", an elegant open gallery in black and white marble from the 1300s. It was from that building that the Captain of the People used to round up the population. In the centre there is a characteristic well dating back to the 1500s. An ancient atmospheric square in the centre of the city.

Basilica of San Nazaro Maggiore

Built around 386 AD by
Sant'Ambrogio, this basilica is
dedicated to the apostles. According
to tradition it contains some relics
that used to belong to them. It is an
important token of early Christian art
but has undergone various changes over
the centuries including having to be
rebuilt after a devastating fire in 1075.
The last of these changes brought
about the discovery of a Romanesque
building from the 9th century, parts
of the early Christian walls and a bas-
relief portraying San Nazaro. There
is a large collection of archeological
remains and works of art conserved
inside the church. The most unusual
feature is that the basilica doesn't have
a main façade and access is through the
Trivulzio Chapel, started in 1512 by
Bramantino and never finished.

Ancient Maggiore Hospital "Ca' Granda"

Also known as "Ca' Granda" (how big), this hospital was built by Francesco Sforza in 1456 of his own free will. It brought all the different hospitals in the city under one roof thus becoming one of the largest and well equipped in Europe. It was built with the participation of several different architects, which accounts for its unusual and suggestive mixture of styles characterized by Gothic and Renaissance elements which can be seen in its long brick façades. In the internal courtyard of the building there is a magnificent lodge. Today it is host to the University of Milan.

1 – "Ca' Granda"
2 – Trivulzio Chapel
3 – The Basilica di San Nazaro Maggiore complex

Valesca Tower

This sky scraper was built between 1956 and 1958. It is 26 floors high and the last 18 floors are wider than the others. The expanding top floors were added to compensate for the limited space available in the square where it was built. It is one of the most outstanding symbols of the city along with such monuments as the Duomo and the Sforzesco Castle. Inside there are shops, offices and apartments.

Below, Piazza Missori with the remains of the ancient early Christian Basilica

Valesca Tower

53

Basilica of Santa Maria della Passione

This Church dates back to the 1500s and is one of the largest (coming second in size after the Duomo) and most beautiful in the city. It was designed and started by Giovanni Battagio, then carried on by Cristoforo Lombardo who completed the

dome in 1530 and the Baroque façade was built from 1629 to 1729 by the architect Rusnati. The inside of the church is a veritable art gallery: there are works by Daniele Crespi, Bernardino Luini, Gaudenzio Ferrari and other artists coming from cultural areas outside Lombardy.

Church of San Pietro in Gessate

Erected near an old convent, this is one of the most important examples of 15th century architecture. It was redone during the Baroque period and has undergone various reconstructions over the centuries. In 1912 the bell tower and the front of the church were restored back to their original forms but the 17th century door with its sculpture of the patron saint has been conserved. Inside there are a large number of frescoes, among which the "Adoration of the Magi" by Gian Battisti Secchi.

The Rotonda Besana

Due to its unusual architecture this is considered to be one of the most original constructions from 18th century Milan. There is a church in its centre surrounded by harmonious porticoes. It was a burial ground until the end of the 18th century, used as a hospital for contagious patients during the smallpox epidemic between 1870 and 1871 and then as a hospital launderette until 1940. Today, after various restoration projects, it is used for cultural and artistic events.

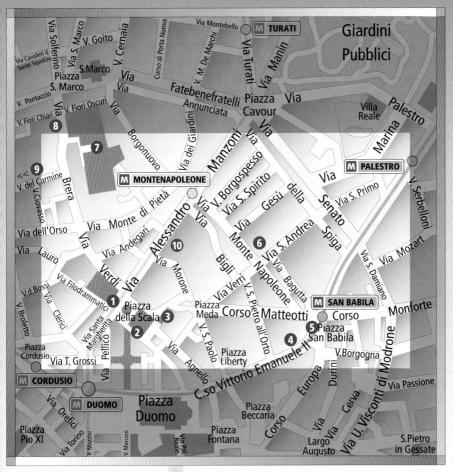

The Scala Theatre

The Scala Theatre was commissioned by the empress Maria Teresa of Austria and was opened on August 3, 1778. It was built by the great neoclassic architect Giuseppe Piermarini with a simple and sober exterior while the interior is decorated

in ivory and red. It can hold up to 2000 spectators and has one of the largest stages in Italy. It is considered the most famous opera house in the world and has always put on very important events with the most acclaimed artists of lyrical and symphonic music.

Piazza della Scala with the Leonardo Monument in its centre

LEONARDO

*Characteristic period tram
in Piazza della Scala*

Palazzo Marino

This palazzo was built in 1558 by Galeazzo Alessi and commissioned by the rich Genovese banker Tommaso Marino (from whom it gets its name). It is one of the most beautiful buildings in Milan and the only one with four faces. The façade that looks onto Piazza della Scala was originally behind the façade that faced the back of Piazza San Fedele and was done by Luca Beltrami in 1889. The exterior represents a balanced synthesis of Renaissance and Baroque styles. The interior courtyard is richly decorated in ornate columns, festoons, niches and statues. The only viewable room is on the ground floor, the "Sala dell'Alessi", with pictorial and stucco decorations.

Piazza and Church of San Fedele

Piazza San Fedele, with its monument dedicated to the famous writer Alessandro Manzoni in the centre, is one of the oldest and most beautiful squares in Milan. It is adorned with two important 16th century monuments: the posterior façade of Palazzo Marino and the Church of San Fedele. The latter was built over the top of the Church of Santa Maria in Solaio and was transformed into its current Baroque style by Carlo Borromeo in 1569, commissioned by a group of Jesuits who wanted to set up their premises there. It has a rigorous and severe shape and the interior is an entire nave distinguished by a series of monumental and very tall columns in red granite.

Corso Vittorio Emanuele II and the Church of San Carlo al Corso

Corso Vittorio Emanuele II is the main high street in the city and unites the Duomo with Piazza San Babila. The wide pedestrian street, rich in shops, bars, cinemas and with porticoes down both sides is one of the most important shopping areas in Milan. Some metres from Piazza San Babila there is a little square on the left where you will find the impressive Church of San Carlo al Corso. It was built between 1839 and 1847 by Carlo Amati in a neoclassic form and was vaguely inspired by the Roman Pantheon. The interior is rich in decoration and works of art.

Corso Vittorio Emanuele II and the Duomo

Piazza San Babila

Piazza and Church of San Babila

Piazza San Babila, rich in shops, theatres and cinemas is one of the most elegant places in the city and was once a common meeting place for the well-to-do of Milan. The Church of San Babila nearly goes unnoticed being completely surrounded by buildings. It is an ancient church that was built on top of the remains of a basilica dating back to the 4th century AD. The 17th century Lion Column can be found in the churchyard: the stone animal was probably a heraldic symbol for the quarter.

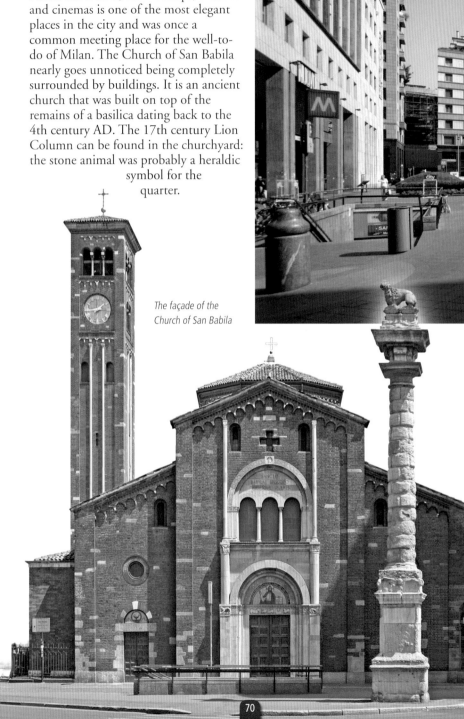

The façade of the Church of San Babila

Fashion District

Via Montenapoleone, Via della Spiga, Via Sant'Andrea together with Via Manzoni, Via Borgospesso and Via Santo Spirito define the well-known "Quadrilatero delle Moda" (Fashion District). Many go there to shop, the Milanese as well as tourists. It is a temple for luxury and quality shopping. All the famous fashion brands can be found: the most prestigious designer clothes, accessories, shoes, jewellery, etc. The zone is sober and elegant with its 19th century architecture and hosts noble and important buildings.

Palazzo di Brera

This is a typical example of Lombard Baroque architecture. It was started in 1627 based on a project by Francesco Maria Richini. It wasn't completed until 1780 by Giuseppe Piermarini who added a magnificent doorway. Inside there is a large

rectangular courtyard surrounded by two rows of arches with a bronze statue of
Napoleon Bonaparte as Mars the Pacifier in the middle from the 19th century
by Canova. The "palazzo" is now home to the Brera Art Gallery, the Belle Arti
Academy, the Braidense National Library and the Astronomic Observatory.

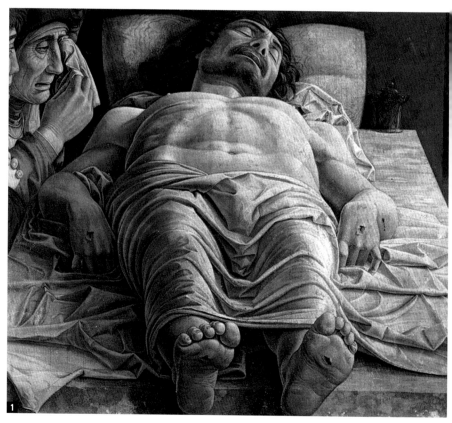

Brera Art Gallery

Inside the noble Palazzo di Brera, where the Belle Arti Academy and the Braidense National Library are also located, the entrance to the Brera Art Gallery is at the top of the large 17th century staircase at the end of the courtyard. Its rich collection is made up of a combination of paintings requisitioned from churches and convents during the Napoleonic period (1798), which renders it one of the main museums in Europe. Once there, one can admire famous pieces like the *Madonna and Child* by Giovanni Bellini, the *Crucifixion* by Bramantino, the *Madonna of the Rosary* by Luini and the *Supper at Emmaus* by Caravaggio. There are also works of art like *Dead Christ* by Mantegna, the *Marriage of the Virgin* by Raffaello and the *Sacred Conversation* by Piero della Francesca. Representing the Fiamminga School from the 17th century there are paintings by Rubens, Joardens, Van Dyke and Rembrandt. Legacies and purchases went on until the end of the Second World War, providing the art gallery with important pieces by Correggio, Pietro Longhi, Piazzatta, Tiepolo, Canaletto and Fattori, not to mention the *Pergola* by Silvestro Lega. The art gallery has been recently enriched with donations by Emilio and Maria Jesi, which include pieces by important artists from the early 1900s like Boccioni, Braque, Carrà, De Pisis, Marino Marini, Modigliani and Morandi.

1 – "Dead Christ" by Mantegna

2 – "Sacred Conversation" by Piero della Francesca

3 – "Supper at Emmaus" by Caravaggio

4 – "The Kiss" by Francesco Hayez

5 – "Marriage of the Virgin" by Raffaello

Brera Quarter

This is an ancient quarter of Milan, rich in historical buildings, criss-crossed by little characteristic paved streets that used to be crowded with horse pulled carts. The various "literature cafès" give the place a sense of history, culture and art and it has always been a favourite location among artists and intellectuals. The area is also loved by the Milanese and visiting tourists because of its array of restaurants, cafès and fashionable bars, not to mention the unusual shops and studios that make Brera an exclusive shopping zone.

Church of Carmine

Gian Galeazzo Visconti had this church built in 1400. Over the centuries it underwent various collapses and restorations and it now has a façade from the end of the 19th century in an imaginative Gothic-Lombard style. Inside there are a lot of 17th century paintings and a beautiful walnut sacristy, which was completed at the end of the 1600s.

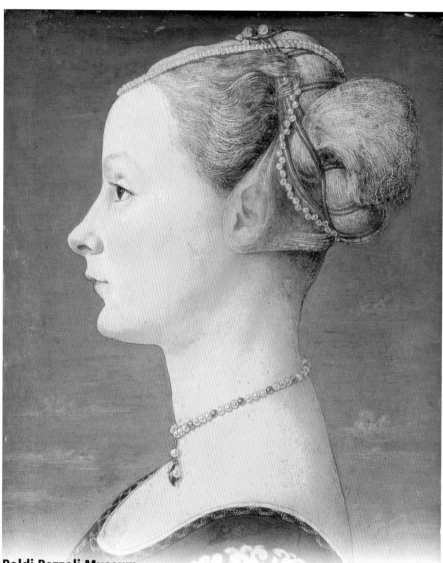

Poldi Pezzoli Museum

House-museum that was created from Gian Giacomo Poldi Pezzoli's private collection, a noble Milanese gentleman who was alive during the 1800s. It has been open to the public since 1881 and offers very high quality and charming pieces, with works of art by great artists like: Piero della Francesca, Botticelli, Pollaiolo, Mantegna, Giovanni Bellini, Carlo Crivelli, Tiepolo, etc. There are also collections of tapestries, lace, furniture and carpets, among which the "Tappeto di caccia" (Hunting Carpet), a Persian work of art, one of the oldest signed and dated (1542-43) in the world. The jewellery is also marvellous. The Weapons Room in the museum has been recently refurbished with an original design by Arnaldo Pomodoro (2000).

The photo shows the painting *Portrait of a Lady* by Pollaiolo.

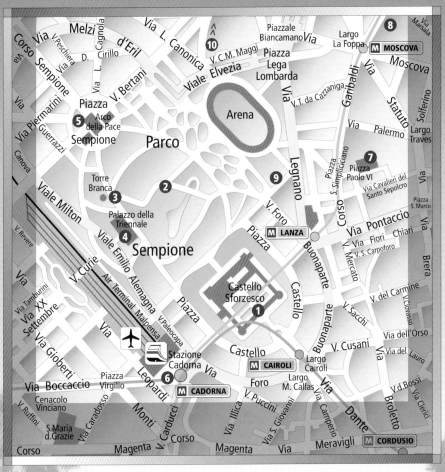

Largo Cairoli, dominated by the Giuseppe Garibaldi monument, which dates back to 1895. In the background, Sforzesco Castle

Sforzesco Castle

This is one of the most important monuments in Milan. It was built for Galeazzo II Visconti in the second half of the 14th century but, starting from 1450, it was reconstructed by Francesco Sforza which set it out to become one of the most beautiful residences in Europe. Between 1480 and 1482 the great artists Leonardo Da Vinci and Bramante were called to Milan to be court artists for Ludovico il Moro. The castle has been through various ups and downs since it was built, among which brutal demolition and rebuilding. Its current appearance is due to a restoration project in the early 20th century which managed to get rid of the military characteristics of the castle, which had since become barracks for the army, and enhance its origins as a noble residence. The central tower (Torre del Filarete), which is facing the city, is the symbol of the castle. It is 70 metres high and was named by the Florentine architect Antonio Averlino known as the "Filarete" who worked on the original tower in the second half of the 15th century. It then collapsed in the 1500s and was rebuilt in 1905 by the architect Luca Beltrami.

Sforzesco Castle as seen from the square
in front with a beautiful fountain

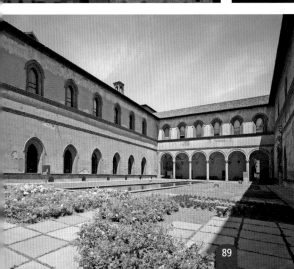

Sforzesco Castle Museum

The castle is embellished with certain treasures collected over the centuries and kept in its museums. At the moment the collection occupies the ground floor of the *Museum of Ancient* Art where the "Sala dell'Asse" can be found with a vault created by Leonardo Da Vinci and the celebrated sculpture of Michelangelo known as "Pietà Rondanini" that the artist was never able to finish (1564). The first floor is occupied by the *Museum of Furniture* with pieces mainly made out of wood, the *Art Gallery* with a rich collection of paintings by artists such as Filippo Lippi, Antonello da Messina, Andrea Mantegna and Canaletto. Part of the first floor and the second floor of the Rocchetta is occupied by the *Museum of Musical Instruments* appreciated for its richness and variety of pieces and the *Raccolte d'arte applicata* (The collection of applied art) containing handmade high quality artistic objects, precious jewellery and scientific instruments. *The Museum of Prehistory and Proto-history* is situated underground in the Ducal Courtyard and is divided into three parts; the Neolithic Age, the Bronze Age, the Iron Age and the *Egyptian Museum*.

1 – Sepulchral monument of Bernabò Visconti (14th century)

2 – 17th century helmets in the Weapons Room

3 – Funereal monument of Gaston de Foix (16th century)

4 – Six-string guitar and two mandolins in the Museum of Musical Instruments

5 – Painting of Gian Galeazzo Maria Sforza (1476)

6 – The "Madonna and saints in glory" by Andrea Mantegna (1497)

7 – "Pietà Rondanini" by Michelangelo (1564)

Sempione Park

Its 47 hectares of land makes this one of the most extensive parks in the centre of the city. It was designed in 1893 by the architect Emilio Alemagna, who specifically wanted to create a perspective game between Sforzesco Castle and the Arch of Peace. Based on a traditional English garden, it is picturesque and full of trees, paths, little bridges, running streams, hills and fountains.

1 – A view of the park with Sforzesco Castle in the background

2 – Next to Sempione Park one can find the Branca Tower Built according to a design by the architect Giò Ponti, it is 108 metres tall and was completed in 1933. Later on it was completely restored by the Branca brothers from whom it gets its name. Thanks to its observation elevator that goes right to the top of the tower, one can enjoy the incredible view of the city's main monuments: the Arch of Peace, Sforzesco Castle and the Duomo

3 – The Triennale Palace holds a very large collection of design objects and hosts a lot of temporary modern art exhibitions. Outside the building one can admire the "Mysterious Bathing" fountain, the last project completed by the famous painter and sculptor Giorgio De Chirico

Arch of Peace

The "Arco della Pace" was created by Luigi Cagnole in 1807 to celebrate Napoleon's victory. Its completion was interrupted by the defeat of the same Napoleon at Waterloo in 1815. Because of this it wasn't officially opened until 1838 and was dedicated to peace after the end of the Napoleonic Age.

It is 25 metres high, done in granite and is made up of three arches with the largest

in the middle, with giant fluted columns resting on bas-relief ornate pedestals. This masterful monument is also characterised by its decorative display: the "Chariot of Peace" by Abbondio Sangiorgio, the "Mounted Victories" by Giovanni Putti and a representation of the four rivers (Po, Ticino, Adige and Tagliamento) in the form of two statues on each side of the arch.

Piazza Cadorna

This square was designed by Gae Aulenti and is one of the main junctions in the centre of the city: in fact, it connects Sforzesco Castle with the painting of The Last Supper and the "Navigli" (canals) as well as hosting Cadorna Railway Station. In

the middle of the square is an enormous sculpture by Claes Oldenburg and his wife Coosje Van Bruggen. It is made of steel and glass resin and represents "A Needle, a Thread and a Knot". Colourful in red, green and yellow like the underground lines, it pays homage to the Milanese for their industriousness and hard work.

Basilica of San Simpliciano

This was one of the first churches built in Milan: in fact, it dates back to the 3rd century AD and was built on top of a pagan cemetery according to analysed marble and stucco discovered around the building. Sant'Ambrogio ordered its construction but the project was terminated by his successor San Simpliciano, who is buried there. The relics of Saints Sisno, Martirio and Alessandro are conserved inside the church, thanks to the intervention which, according to tradition, saw the Lombard League win the battle of Legnano in 1176 against Federico Barbarossa (some scenes are represented in the windows on the front of the church). It has undergone various changes over the centuries but thanks to recent restoration projects parts of the early Christian structure have been revealed, giving the church back some of its original Romanesque features.

Church of Santa Maria Incoronata

Santa Maria Incoronata is two churches in one. The first, the one on the left, was an ancient little church that was later restored in a late Gothic style. The completion of the work coincided with the coronation of Francesco Sforza (1451), who it is dedicated to. Nine years later, Sforza's wife Bianca Maria Visconti, had a second identical church built attached to the original in order to create one church demonstrating the union of their two families, no more divided by war. As well as its beautiful architectural features, it also contains various works of art by famous painters. Recent restoration work has brought to light the ancient Humanistic Library.

The City Aquarium was built in 1906 and is one of the oldest aquariums in the world. A long restoration project has returned the outside of the building to its original splendour, while the interior is rich in decoration and contains 32 pools. The aquarium offers a detailed view of Italian aquatic life in both fresh and salt water. At the end of the tour there is a large terrarium where one can see numerous amphibians hidden in the vegetation

Monumental Cemetery

This is a magnificent cemetery situated in the centre of the city. It was designed by the architect Carlo Maciachini and opened in 1866. Over the years it has gradually been filled with classic and modern sculptures from Greek temples and obelisks and other original pieces such as a small version of the Traiano Column. It is considered to be an open air museum, witness to events that have taken place in the city and colourful lives that have made history.

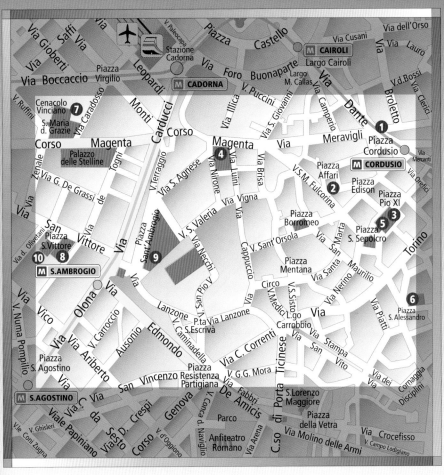

Piazza Cordusio

This square is surrounded by financial institutions and a wide variety of shops. It was completed at the end of the 1800s in order to regularise the quarter. From here one can enjoy a suggestive view of the Duomo on one side and Sforzesco Castle on the other.

1 | 2 | 3 – View of Piazza Cordusio crossed by characteristic period trams

4 – Piazza Affari is Milan's financial hub and faces the Stock Exchange building, which was built in 1931. The façade is in travertine and the interior is host to a vast stock exchange hall

Via Dante, pedestrian area surrounded by noble buildings and a particularly pleasant walk from the Duomo to Sforzesco Castle

Ambrosiana Art Gallery

The Ambrosiana Art Gallery was founded by Federico Borromeo in 1618 who donated his own private collection of paintings as a starting point. Here one can admire unique and precious works of Italian and international art.

The Art Gallery now holds more than 1500 pieces. Among the most famous one can see: the *Portrait of a Musician* by Leonardo Da Vinci, the *Fruit Basket* by Caravaggio, the *Portrait of a Lady* by Giovanni Ambrogio De Predis, the "*Madonna del padiglione*" by Botticelli, the *Nativity* by Barocci, the *Adoration of the Magi* by Tiziano, the *Holy Family* by Luini, *Fire and Water* by Brueghel and the large cartoon by Raffaello named *School of Athens*.

The Ambrosiana Library is an integral part of the art gallery and was also founded by Borromeo in 1609. It contains rare and important manuscripts among which the very famous *Codex Atlanticus* by Leonardo.

On the opposite page: "Portrait of Musician" by Leonardo Da Vinci

1 – "Fruit Basket" by Caravaggio

2 – "Portrait of a Lady" by Giovanni Ambrogio De Predis

Church of San Maurizio al Monastero Maggiore

This is a splendid church, which was built from 1503 onwards inside the Benedictine Monastery. Its sober exterior contrasts with the interior, which is richly decorated in gold. It is divided into two parts with one section dedicated to the congregation and the other reserved for the nuns.

It is entirely frescoed with wonderful cycles of paintings created by the most important artists from 16th century Lombardy. It also contains a prestigious organ from 1554. The foundations of the square bell tower are the remains of a Roman circus that used to be situated there. One of the two cloisters is used as an Archaeological Museum.

Church of San Sepolcro

This church was founded around 1100 with similar style to the Holy Sepulchre in Jerusalem. Over the years it has undergone various rearrangements. The bell towers were added in 1200 and the façade was rebuilt in 1800. Inside, two groups of terracotta statues from the 16th century are conserved. In Roman times, the square was situated where the two main streets (the Cardo and the Decumanus) crossed and also where the Forum was held.

Church of Sant'Alessandro

Built in 1602 based on a project by Lorenzo Birago, it is one of the most beautiful examples of Baroque architecture in the city. Inside, one can admire canvases by Camillo Procaccini and Daniele Crespi. It is situated very near to Via Torino in a not very well-known but suggestive piazza in the old part of Milan. It is surrounded by period buildings, untouched by the tragic bombardments of 1943.

Church of Santa Maria delle Grazie

Church of Santa Maria delle Grazie

This church was built between 1464 and 1482 based on a project by the architect Guiniforte Solari. It later underwent various important modifications ordered by Ludovico il Moro, who decided to turn it into a sepulchral monument for his family. As a result, various prestigious artists were called upon among whom Bramante, who, inspired by the new renaissance dictates, rebuilt the wonderful gallery, the cloister and the Old Sacristy. In the refectory, Leonardo Da Vinci completed one of the most celebrated masterpieces in the world: The Last Supper. Since 1980, the church and The Last Supper have been part of UNESCO.

The Cenacle (The Last Supper)

It is universally known as "The Last Supper" and was painted by **Leonardo Da Vinci** during the reign of Ludovico il Moro between 1494 and 1498. The most symbolic of all Leonardo's great pieces and it took him a long time to finish. This is because instead of using traditional fresco techniques, he adopted a "dry" technique, which allowed substantial changes to be made throughout the making. Represented in the piece are the apostles and Jesus at the moment he announced there was a traitor among them. All the drama of that moment is expressed in the painting, seen in the facial expressions, the gestures and the character's postures. The positioning of the figures, with Jesus in the middle and the apostles put into groups of three, was created with mathematic precision and great composite harmony and represents an absolute novelty in the striking realism with which the scene is narrated.

There were, however, flaws in the technique used by Leonardo and these became clear when the masterpiece began to deteriorate only a few years after its completion. It miraculously escaped the bombardments of 1943, which destroyed most of the refectory. It has been the object of various restoration works, the latest of which finished in 1999, was carried out using the most up-to-date scientific methods and reinstated luminosity and chromatic freshness that was unimaginable some ten years ago.

The "Leonardo Da Vinci" National Museum of Science and Technology

Situated in a 16th century Olivetan Monastery in the heart of Milan, it is the largest scientific and technical museum in Italy covering a total surface area of 40,000 square metres. It is named after Leonardo Da Vinci, who managed to bring together art, science and technology, and contains more than 10,000 objects that demonstrate scientific and technological development in Italy. Next to the exhibition area, various interactive laboratories (i.lab) have been added which provide informal learning for anyone interested, including schools, families and the general public. The collections and laboratories are organised into six departments: Materials, Transport, Energy, Communication, Leonardo Art and Science, and New Frontiers. In 2005 the museum enriched its collection with the arrival of the Enrico Toti Submarine S 506, which can be explored inside with a scientific guide.

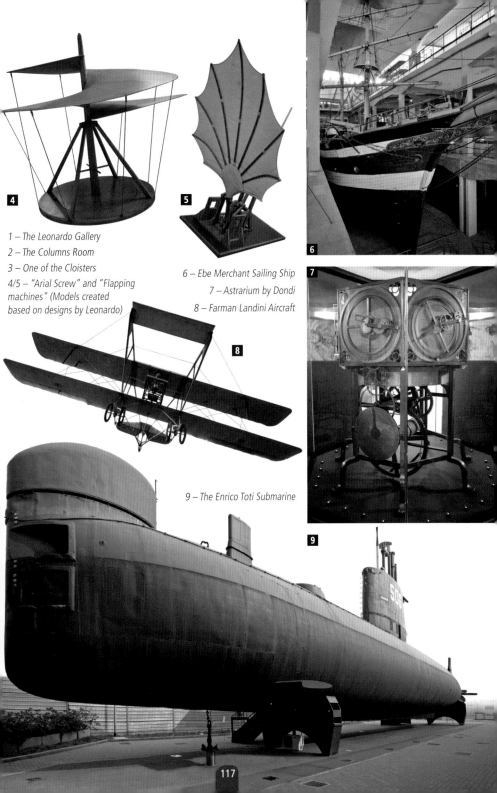

1 – The Leonardo Gallery
2 – The Columns Room
3 – One of the Cloisters
4/5 – "Arial Screw" and "Flapping machines" (Models created based on designs by Leonardo)

6 – Ebe Merchant Sailing Ship
7 – Astrarium by Dondi
8 – Farman Landini Aircraft

9 – The Enrico Toti Submarine

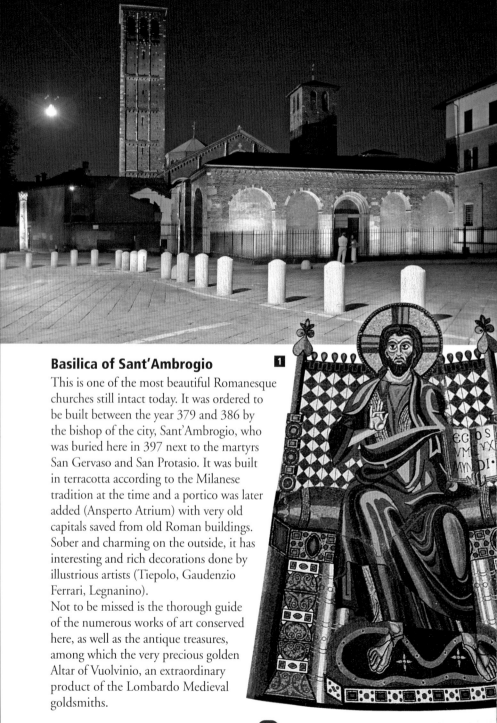

Basilica of Sant'Ambrogio **1**

This is one of the most beautiful Romanesque churches still intact today. It was ordered to be built between the year 379 and 386 by the bishop of the city, Sant'Ambrogio, who was buried here in 397 next to the martyrs San Gervaso and San Protasio. It was built in terracotta according to the Milanese tradition at the time and a portico was later added (Ansperto Atrium) with very old capitals saved from old Roman buildings. Sober and charming on the outside, it has interesting and rich decorations done by illustrious artists (Tiepolo, Gaudenzio Ferrari, Legnanino).

Not to be missed is the thorough guide of the numerous works of art conserved here, as well as the antique treasures, among which the very precious golden Altar of Vuolvinio, an extraordinary product of the Lombardo Medieval goldsmiths.

1 – The great apsidal mosaic as it is seen today. It is the result of various restoration projects that makes it very difficult to place chronologically. The central part that makes up the figure of Christ reveals a late Byzantine matrix and can be dated back to the beginning of the 13th century, whereas the lateral design can even be dated back to the Carolingian Age around the 9th century

3 – The inside of the basilica

2 – The Serpent of Moses: a bronze sculpture situated inside the basilica on a granite column. In the past it was believed to be the sculpture forged by Moses himself to protect his camp from the desert snakes. The statue is connected to popular belief about the end of the world previously announced by the serpent's descent from the column

4 – The "Sacellum of San Vittore in the Golden Sky" was created in the 4th century, before the basilica itself and is a very rare example of early Christian art in Milan. Bishop Materno wished for it to be built in order to house the spoils of Martyr Vittore. Legend has it that Ambrogio placed the remains of Brother Satiro here around the year 375. The wonderful mosaic dates back to the 5th century and is the oldest known image of Sant'Ambrogio and its realism is impressive

Above, the Altar of Vuolvinio dating back to the 9th century gets its name from its creator and contains the relics of Sant'Ambrogio, San Protasio and San Gervaso. The panels pair together the stories of the lives of Jesus and Sant'Ambrogio himself and they are a very important example of Medieval goldsmith's art

Above, a detail of the sarcophagus named "Stilicone" after the Roman general who died in 408 AD and is believed to be buried here

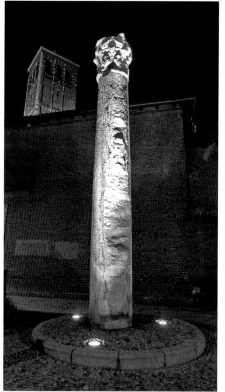

On the Left, the Devil's Column situated outside the basilica. This is a Roman Column with two holes: legend has it that the Devil, while trying to dissuade Sant'Ambrogio to take on his role as bishop, started to fight with him and during the struggle, his horns were driven into the column. Stuck there until the following day, he disappeared through one of the holes opening up a passage to hell. According to legend, the holes smell of sulphur and if you put your ear up against the column, you can hear noises coming from hell

The front of the Church of Sant'Ambrogio faces the Ansperto Atrium and is dominated by two bell towers: the lower one called "dei Monaci" (of the Monks), dates back to the 9th century, the taller one, known as "dei Canonici" (of the Canons), was built in the 12th century

Church of San Vittore al Corpo

This church is of early Christian origin and was built in the 4th century over the remains of an Imperial Roman Mausoleum. It was completely redone in the 16th century. The façade is linear and simple, while the interior is complex and articulate with a richly decorated vault.

On the right, the "Pusterla di Sant'Ambrogio". It was built in 1939 as an imitation of a door in the ancient medieval walls in the original materials.
The tabernacle with the Ambrogio Saints Gervasio and Protasio dating back to the 15th century

Basilica of San Lorenzo Maggiore

This is the most important example of early Christian architecture in Milan. It has survived the centuries practically intact despite undergoing numerous restorations. The original structure dates back to the 4th century, the façade is from the 1800s, the majestic cupola is from 1573 and is the largest in Milan. The interior, today all one

colour and lit up like a theatre, used to be multicoloured and sumptuously furnished. There are other chapels connected to the body of the basilica. One in particular, dedicated to Sant'Aquilino, contains precious mosaics from the 4th century that adorn the vault. In front of the church stands a statue of the Emperor Constantine.

Columns of San Lorenzo

16 marble columns fluted with Corinthian capitals, salvaged from a Roman temple, form the front of this impressive four-sided-portico of the Basilica of San Lorenzo. This place is loved by the Milanese because of its suggestiveness and breathtaking

atmosphere. In the centre of the square there is a bronze copy of the Statue of Emperor Constantine, made from the original dating back to the 4th century that can be found in San Giovanni in Laterano in Rome.

Piazza Vetra

From here one can admire the back of the Basilica of San Lorenzo with its chapels and towers. There was once a canal instead of the square and the remains of a Roman bridge from the 3rd century were found here. From the middle of the 9th century, for about 800 years, it was used for capital punishment and was famous for being ill-omened for a long time.

Basilica of Sant'Eustorgio

This is one of the most important monumental complexes in the city and was founded in the 4th century by Sant'Eustorgio. Inside the basilica there are numerous eight-pointed stars that represent the Three Wise Men: legend has it that they were buried here until 1164 when their remains were taken away by Federico Barbarossa. Some of these alleged relics were then returned in 1903 and are now conserved in

a special urn in the Chapel of the Three Wise Men. The church, rich in precious works of art including 14th century frescoes in the fourth chapel, is one of the most important work of art from the Lombard Renaissance. The bell tower is also of interest and dates back to 1190. It is the tallest in Milan (75 metres) and was the first in the city to be endowed with a clock in 1306. The museum and the Portinari Chapel behind the apse are worth visiting.

Portinari Chapel

Adjacent to the Basilica of Sant'Eustorgio there is an architectural gem from the Renaissance period. It dates back to the 15th century and it stands out because of a decorative system designed at the same time as and in unison with the architecture. The decorations by Vincenzo Foppa are delicate and innovative: his set of frescoes dedicated to San Pietro the Martyr was miraculously salvaged during the latest restoration work following various ups and downs over the course of the centuries. The cupola, hidden under nearly seven layers of plaster during the plague of 1630, can now be seen in all its original splendour. One can admire the extraordinary beauty of the luminous vault painted with a scaled pattern in bright colours. In its centre there is a 14th century marble arch by Giovanni di Balduccio, in which the relics of the martyr are contained.

Church of San Celso and Santa Maria dei Miracoli

Legend has it that the Church of San Celso (right-hand photo) was erected over the spot where Sant'Ambrogio found the relics of Nazaro and Celso. It was built in the 4th century in order to protect an effigy of the Madonna situated on the spot where the bodies were found. It was then rebuilt in a Romanesque style in the 11th century. The large influx of believers coming to venerate the holy effigy brought about the decision to build the adjacent Basilica of Santa Maria dei Miracoli (the

church on the left), a majestic building designed by Giangiacomo Dolcebuono at the end of the 15th century that took about a century to complete. The entrance is preceded by a porticoed atrium, while the interior itself is adorned with golden coffered ceilings, refined floors made of Candoglia marble (the same as the Duomo), numerous frescoes and altar pieces by Lombardo artists from the Renaissance and the Baroque period.

The "Navigli"

The "Navigli" (canals) were built in the 15th century by the Duke of Milan, Ludovico Sforza, with a view to allowing access to the city from Ticino as well as Adda. These waterways were based on an exclusive design by Leonardo Da Vinci to level out the land and allow navigation. A large amount of commodities were transported through these canals including marble from Candoglia (near Lake Maggiore) used for the construction of the Duomo. Merchants stopped using the

canals as a means of transport in the second half of the 1800s and slow navigation was replaced by railways and tramways. Today, the canal area contains some of the most popular bars in Milan and, especially during the summer, it's a hot spot for tourists and Milanese, who are attracted to the timeless atmosphere only a few minutes from the city centre. There is a traditional market every Saturday (Fiera di Sinigallia) and, every last Sunday of the month there is a not-to-be-missed antiques market for those passionate collectors.

1 – Bridge over the Naviglio Grande

2 – Darsena

3 – Naviglio Grande at sunset

4 – Characteristic bars on Naviglio Pavese

5 – A Canal lock (Conca del Naviglio)

1

Church of San Cristoforo sul Naviglio

The church (photo 1) is situated in a once suburban area along the left bank of the Naviglio Grande (main canal). The building is actually made up of two churches: the older one dates back to the 13th century with a Gothic front door and a rose window added in the middle of the 14th century; the most recently built of the two called Cappella Ducale (Ducal Chapel) dates back to the 15th century. It was built as a result of a vow made by the population to San Cristoforo, protector of travellers and wayfarers, during the plague. Inside one can admire frescoes from the Bergognone and Luini School.

3

1 – The Church of San Cristoforo sul Naviglio
2 – Naviglio Grande
3 – The characteristic Vicolo dei Lavandai
(laundress lane)

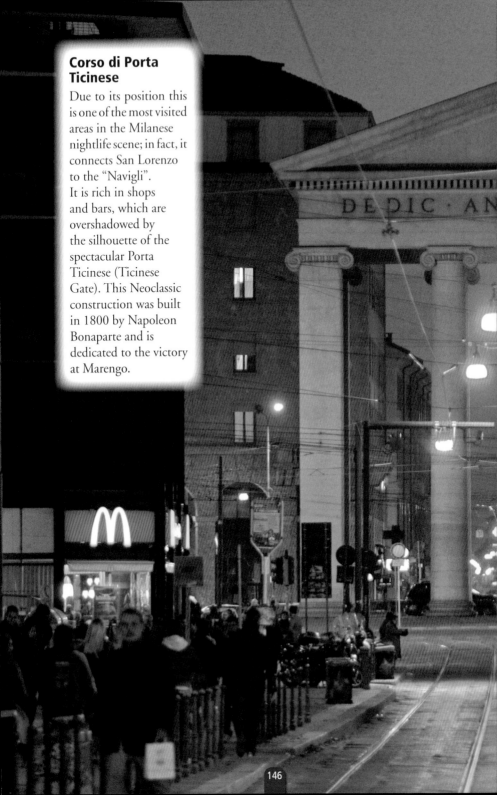

Corso di Porta Ticinese

Due to its position this is one of the most visited areas in the Milanese nightlife scene; in fact, it connects San Lorenzo to the "Navigli".
It is rich in shops and bars, which are overshadowed by the silhouette of the spectacular Porta Ticinese (Ticinese Gate). This Neoclassic construction was built in 1800 by Napoleon Bonaparte and is dedicated to the victory at Marengo.

Roman Amphitheatre

The amphitheatre in Milan (photo above) was built outside the city walls and because of its considerable size it is one of the most impressive pieces of architecture in the city. Today, despite being one of the largest amphitheatres in the Roman Empire, there are only a few visible remains left in the Amphitheatre Park and Via Conca del Naviglio

The Medieval Porta Ticinese was one of the doors on the outskirts of Milan, sheltered by the Columns of San Lorenzo. It was erected in 1171 but owes its current form to work carried out in the 1800s

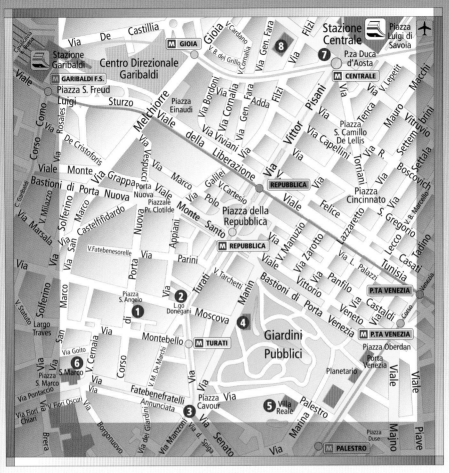

1

Church of Sant'Angelo

Built in the second half of the 16th century with a façade that was completed a century later, this is one of the few churches in Milan that hasn't been drastically altered and can be admired in its original Baroque state. The interior is richly decorated and the side chapels have been preserved well with canvases dating back to the 1500s and 1600s. (photo 1)

2

2 – Palazzo Dugnani, a large residency from the 17th century. Inside it contains frescoes by Tiepolo, Ferdinando Porta and the School of Veneto. Today it is the Cinema Museum

3/4 –The Arches of Porta Nuova are part of a circle of walls built in 1162. Made of black and white marble, the two arches were once flanked with towers and the marble tabernacle representing Our Lady with Child was added between 1330 and 1339. There are also two Roman memorial stones set in the arches dating back to the 1st century AD (photo 3)

5 – The "Cà Brutta" was created by the architect Giovanni Muzio in 1918. Its unusual shape was an attempt at bringing together historical tradition and modern innovation together with functionality. However, people didn't understand the inspiration behind its design and it was soon known as "Cà Brutta" (How ugly)

Villa Reale (Royal Villa)

The Royal Villa was built between 1790 and 1793 by the architect Leopoldo Pollack for Count Ludovico Barbiano di Belgioioso. It was then bought by the Cisalpine Republic, which gave it to Napoleon Bonaparte. Later on it was home to Viceroy

Eugenio Beauharnais and then General Radetzky. It is one of the most important examples of Milanese Neoclassicism. The posterior façade is particularly impressive, which faces the suggestive English gardens. The interior is rich in frescoes, sculptures, furniture and various objects. Today it is a Modern Art Gallery.

Church of San Marco

This building dates back to 1199 and was named San Marco as a mark of respect to the Venetians who helped the Milanese rebuild the city after the period of fighting against Federico Barbarossa. Rebuilt in 1250, the church is fundamentally Gothic but there is evidence of other eras: the bell tower dates back to the 13th century, the Neo-gothic façade still contains some 14th century sculptures and the sequence of chapels on the right hand side were built between the 16th and 18th century. The Baroque interior is embellished with wonderful frescoes. Mozart (1770) stayed in the canonical of this church and in 1874, the Requiem Mass, conducted by Verdi, was performed for the first time in memory of the writer Alessandro Manzoni.

Central Station

This is one of the most important and magnificent stations in Europe. It was designed by Ulisse Stacchini in 1912 but its construction wasn't started until 1926 and finished in 1932. It is very representative of the fascist regime. This can be seen in the huge frontal body that is 207 metres long. Made of stone and marble, there is a mixture of styles, among the most prominent, Art deco and Liberty.

Pirelli Skyscraper

Also known as "Pirellone" because it soars out of the first Pirelli factory, it is 127 metres high and the second tallest skyscraper in Italy next to the Telecom Tower in Naples. It was designed by Gio Ponti and was built between 1956 and 1961. It is now host to the Lombardy Region offices.

Milan and the surrounding area

Chiaravalle Abbey

This important Cistercian Monastery is situated on the outskirts of Milan (5 km from the city). It was founded in 1135 by San Bernardo di Clairvaux, from whom the Italianised name comes. Built in a swampy area and drained by the monks, it became one of the most important centres for artists and religious followers at the time. The tower, splendid and linear, dates back to 1347 and is made of red brick that contrasts against the white of the arches. The interior has a nave and two aisles and is embellished with frescoes by Tuscan artists dating back to the first half of the 1300s (the Cycle of the Story of the Virgins). Other works of art include pieces by Fiammenghini (16th and 17th century). Also of interest is the 17th century wooden Choir Pit created by the great carver, Carlo Garavaglia. According to legend, he took refuge here and carved the splendid work of art in order to expiate his guilt for murdering one of his siblings. Next to the church there is an ancient cemetery, connected to the Gothic cloister, which overlook the refectory (14th century) and the Capitulary Room.

Carthusian Monastery (Certosa) of Garegnano

Situated in the suburbs of Milan, the area in which it was built was once open countryside to allow the monks to live in peace and quiet. It was founded in 1349 by Giovanni Visconti and became a place of rest for pilgrims, wayfarers and illustrious characters like the poet Francesco Petrarca, who often mentioned the monastery describing it as "beautiful and noble". Today, the complex comprises the Church of Santa Maria Assunta and holds many valued decorations, statues

bas-reliefs, preceded by two courtyards and the Cloister, which used to contain the Monks' cells, the Refectory and the Capitulary Room. Next to these you will find the working area with the stables, the ovens, the press etc. The monastery is, however, renowned for its precious frescoes, original works of art from the 16th and 17th centuries by Simone Peterzano, famous as the teacher of Caravaggio and Daniele Crespi. In the vault of the Capitulary Room there is a beautiful fresco of San Michele by Bernardo Zenale.

Arcimboldi Theatre

This was designed by Vittorio Gregoretti, was opened in 2002 and can hold 2,400 spectators. It is an exclusive structure in Milan because of its innovative building criteria, acoustics and visuals. The size and shape of the stage is very similar to that of the Scala Theatre, allowing scenes to be transferred between the two theatres. It is situated in the Bicocca quarter between the urban centre and the metropolitan area, which renders it easily accessible from the city centre as well as the outskirts. (Right-hand photo)

Bovisa Quarter

The Bovisa Quarter is an old and historical area on the border of Northern Milan in an industrialised area rich in factories that were closed at the end of the 70s turning it into a dormitory suburb. The area was upgraded with the opening of the Polytechnic (left-hand photo) in the 80s followed by the creation of one of the most prestigious university districts in Italy. Today, over 200,000 people go to the area everyday and it has become the symbol of the rebirth and improvement of the suburbs. Full of events, demonstrations and shows, it is an increasingly popular destination for artists who choose to open their studios there. Since 2006 it has been the location for the "Triennale Bovisa", an area entirely dedicated to contemporaneity through decidedly avant-garde art exhibitions.

Fieramilano (Exhibition Centre of Milan)

The new exhibition centre in Milan was opened in 2005 and is situated in Rho. Fieramilano is one of the most modern, advanced and functional international exhibition centres that exist today. In fewer than three years, the innovative project by the architect Massimiliano Fuksas has become an avant-garde exhibition complex hosting important international events. The area unites supreme dimensions with exceptional utilisation flexibility, aesthetics and comfort, high level technological equipment and maximum accessibility of space. There are eight pavilions in the quarter with a total exhibiting surface area of 345,000 square-metres and an extra 60.000 square-metres of open-air exhibition space. The most distinctive architectural aspect of this complex is the "sail", a structure made of glass and steel measuring 1,300 metres in length, 32 metres in width and 23 metres in height.

1 **San Siro Museum**

This is a must for football lovers. It is the only museum in Italy that has been set up inside a stadium.

It traces the history of the Milanese football teams, Inter and Milan, and also contains a large collection of unique memorabilia: cups, trophies, footballs, football boots, and all

San Siro "Giuseppe Meazza" Stadium

Opened in 1926, the stadium owes its name, San Siro, to the area in which it was built. Both Milanese teams play here: Inter and Milan and it is dedicated to Giuseppe Meazza, a very important Inter captain and world champion with the Italian national team in 1934 and 1938. It has 86,000 sheltered seats. Considered one of the most beautiful stadiums in Europe it is nicknamed "The Scala Theatre to football".

The Inter (photo 1) and Milan (photo 2) changing rooms can be visited through the San Siro Museum

kinds of objects that have become important to the legend of football like shirts worn by Pelè, Maradona, Zidane and Crujiff. Don't miss the room of life-size statues representing some of the most important champions: from Matthäus to Van Basten, from Rummenigge to Gullit and many more.

Horse of Leonardo

This is the largest equestrian monument in the world. It was designed by Leonardo Da Vinci who, however, only managed to create a clay model of it. Charles Dent, an American pilot, tried to have to model completed in 1977 but wasn't able due

to lack of funds. It was finished by the American sculptress Nina Akamu in 1999 and donated to the city. The enormous statue is at the entrance to the San Siro Hippodrome.

Photo Gallery

Enrico Aretini

A view of Piazza del Duomo

Sant'Ambrogio

The Horse of Leonardo Da Vinci

An apse of the Church of Santa Maria delle Grazie

A picturesque view of the Brera Quarter

San Lorenzo

Finally in Piazza del Duomo

The towers of Sant'Ambrogio

Castello Sforzesco

The "Grande Naviglio" (Main Canal)

Solitude at sunset on the spires of the Duomo

Pirelli Skyscraper

House of the Omenoni (Via degli Omenoni)

Sun set on the Main Canal (The "Grande Naviglio")

Piazza San Babila

Sunset on the cupola of San Lorenzo

Portinari Chapel (Basilica of Sant'Eustorgio)

The spires of the Duomo

Constantine dominates the Columns of San Lorenzo

Needle and Thread in Piazza Cadorna

Climbing to the top of the Duomo

Lardo Cairoli with Garibaldi and Castello Sforzesco

Early evening in Corso Vittorio Emanuele II

Fuksas' 'vela' at the exhibition centre in Rho

Vittorio Emanuele II Gallery

Businessmen in Piazza San Babila

Piazza Missori

The fountains in front of Castello Sforzesco

Napoleon in the middle of Piazza di Brera

A surprising view of the underground exit at Missori: look up and you will see the Valesca Tower

The spires of the Duomo

The Columns of San Lorenzo

Portinari Chapel and the bell tower of Sant'Eustorgio

Leonardo keeping watch over the Scala

Moses' serpent (Sant'Ambrogio)

Tram crossing Piazza Cordusio

Characteristic stained-glass window of the Duomo

Plastic display at the Stazione Centrale

Vittorio Emanuele II Gallery

Fountains at Castello Sforzesco

The "Disc" by Arnaldo Pomodoro

Useful Numbers

Emergency Services
Carabinieri 112
State police 113
Local police 02.77271
Fire Brigade 115

Transport
Milano Malpensa and Linate Airports 02.74852200
Orio al Serio Bergamo Airport 035.326323
Main Airlines
Air Canada 800.71779887
Air France 848.884466
Air One 199.207080
Alitalia 06.2222
British Airways 199.712266
Continental 02.69633256
Delta Airlines..800.477.999
Easy Jet 848.887.766
Egypt Air 02.86.5777
Emirates 06.54220213
Flybe 00.44.1392.268529
Japan Airlines...848.874700
Lufthansa 199.400044
US Airways 848.813177

Railway Stations
Stazione Centrale - Piazza Duca d'Aosta 892021
Porta Garibaldi - Piazza Sigmund Freud 892021
Ferrovie Nord - Stazione Cadorna 199.151152

ATM (Milan Transport Company) 800.808181
Radiobus 02.48034803
Taxi .... 02.8585 - 02.4040 - 02.6969

Health
Ambulance 118
Emergency Pharmacy 800.801185
On-duty Doctor 02.345.67

Museums, monuments and places of interest in the city
City Aquarium, V.le Gadio 2 .... 02.88465750
The Last Supper "Cenacolo" by Leonardo Da Vinci
    P.za Santa Maria d. Grazie 02.89421146
Antonio Mazzotta Foundation 02.878197
Arnaldo Pomodoro Foundation, V. Solari 35 ....02.89075394
Castello Sforzesco Museums, P.za Castello 3.............02.88463700
Bagatti Valsecchi Museum, V. Santo Spirito 10 ....02.76006132
City Museum of Natural History, C.so Venezia55.....02.88463280
Cinema Museum, V. Manin 2/B - Pal. Dugnani.........02.6554977
San Siro Stadium "Inter and Milan" Museum
    V. Piccolomini 5 - Stadio San Siro, ingresso 14 ....02.4042432
Basilica of Sant'Ambrogio Museum
    P.za Sant'Ambrogio 15..02.86450895
Museum of Milan, V. Sant'Andrea 6...................... 02.88465933
Museum of Sant'Eustrogio and Portinari Chapel
    P.za Sant'Eustorgio 1 ....02.58101583
Diocesan Museum, C.so Porta Ticinese 95 ....02.89404728
Minguzzi Foundation Museum, V. Palermo 11.........02.36565441
Treccani Foundation Museum, V. Porta 5 .... 02.6572627

"Leonardo Da Vinci" National Museum of Science
    and Technology, V. San Vittore 21 ....02.485551
Poldi Pezzoli Museum, V. Manzoni 12 .... 02.796334
PAC - Padiglione d'Arte Contemporanea
    V. Palestro 14... 02.76020400
Palazzo Reale and Museum of Contemporary Art
    P.za Duomo 12 .... 02.72524301
Ambrosiana Art Gallery, P.za Pio XI 2 ....02.806921
Brera Art Gallery, V. Brera 28 ....02.722631
Hoepli Planetarium, C.so Venezia 57 ....02.88463340
Belle Arti Permanente Society, V. Turati 34 ....02.6599803
Scala Theatre Museum, P.za della Scala 02.72003744
Arcimboldi Theatre
    Quartiere Bicocca, V.le dell'Innovazione 1 ....02.641142200
Triennale Bovisa, V. Lambruschini 31 .... 02.36577801
Triennale of Milano, V.le Alemagna 6 ....02.724341
Veneranda Factory of the Duomo, V. Arcivescovado 1 ..02.860358
Villa Reale and Museum of Modern Art
    V. Palestro 16 ....02.76002819

Churches
Duomo .... Piazza del Duomo
San Babila .... Piazza San Babila
San Carlo al Corso ....Piazza San Carlo (C.so Vitt Emanuele II)
San Cristoforo sul Naviglio .... Via San Cristoforo 3
San Fedele .... Piazza San Fedele
San Gottardo .... Via Francesco Pecorari 2
San Lorenzo Maggiore .... Corso di Porta Ticinese 39
San Marco .... Via San Marco 2
San Maurizio .... Corso Magenta 15
San Nazaro Maggiore .... Piazza San Nazaro in Brolo
San Pietro in Gessate .... Via San Pietro in Gessate
San Sebastiano .... Via Torino 28
San Sepolcro .... Piazza San Sepolcro
San Simpliciano .... Piazza San Simpliciano
San Vittore .... Piazza San Vittore
Sant'Alessandro .... Piazza Sant'Alessandro
Sant'Ambrogio .... Piazza Sant'Ambrogio
Sant'Angelo .... Piazza Sant'Angelo
Sant'Eustorgio .... Piazza Sant'Eustorgio
Santa Maria dei Miracoli presso San Celso .... Corso Italia 37
Santa Maria della Passione .... Via Conservatorio
Santa Maria delle Grazie .... Piazza Santa Maria delle Grazie
Santa Maria Incoronata .... Corso Giuseppe Garibaldi 116
Santa Maria at San Satiro .... Via Torino 19
Certosa (Carthusian Monastery) of Garegnano . Via Garegnano 32
Churches and Monuments outside Milan
Chiaravalle Abbey .... Via S. Arialdo 102 - Milano - 02-57403404
Mirasole Abbey .... Opera (MI) - 02.55038311
Viboldone Abbey .... San Giuliano Milanese (MI) - 02.9841203

Fiere e business
Stock Exchange Building .... Piazza Affari 6 - 02.802871
Fiera Milano .... Rho (MI) - 02.49971

Internet
Milan City Council .... www.comune.milano.it
Lombardy Region .... www.regione.lombardia.it
Malpensa and Linate Airports .... www.sea-aeroportimilano.it
Orio al Serio Airport .... www.sacbo.it
Fiera Milano .... www.fieramilano.it

Many thanks to:
Ambrosiana Art Gallery
Basilica of Sant'Ambrogio Museum
Brera Art Gallery
Castello Sforzesco Museum
Fiera Milano
"Leonardo Da Vinci" National Museum of Science and Technology
Museum of Sant'Eustrogio and Portinari Chapel
Poldi-Pezzoli Museum
San Siro Stadium "Inter and Milan" Museum
The Last Supper "Cenacolo" by Leonardo Da Vinci

comunicazione
Turin - Italy
www.aros-comunicazione.com
aros.comunicazione@tin.it

Photos
Enrico Aretini

Editing
Patrizia Rosso

English Translation   *Spanish Translation*   *Russian Translation*
Chloe Mackin   **Isabel Álvarez Fernández**   **Tamara Iunichina**

Printing
Litograf Editor
Città di Castello (PG) Italy, +39 075.8511344
www.litografeditor.it
final printing: march 2008

ISBN: 978-88-902759-1-3